# Rental Property Investing:

*How to Build and Manage Your Real Estate Empire as well as Creating Passive Income with Rental Properties*

*By Brandon Anderson*

# Table of Contents

## RENTALS IN AN EXPENSIVE MARKET?

# Introduction

Congratulations on downloading Rental Property Investing and thank you for doing so.

The following chapters will discuss everything that you need to know to begin with this kind of investment opportunity. You can choose from many other investments. You can choose for the stock market, flipping homes, starting a business, helping others put up one, or growing your personal retirement account. But none of them provides you with such unique opportunities and as much potential profit without all the volatility and risk as rental properties.

This guidebook will spend some time looking at rental properties and how you can start this kind of investment on your own. We will look at some of the basics and why this is a great option for an investor, some of the risks you may face, why you need some important people on your team and the different types of properties where you can invest in.

From here, we will move on to some of the steps that you need to get a property and to start the investment. First, we will explore how you can get the financing to buy that property before moving on to the steps of purchasing it, selecting the right tenants, working to maintain and renovate it, and even how to exit the investment when you decide it is time.

Rental property investing is not for everyone. Some people find it as too much work as a landlord and to keep up with demands of a rental property while they take care of their own job and home as well. But for those who want to build up their own empire and are not scared to get to work, rental property is the best investment choice out there. This guidebook will provide you with all the tools that you need to get started with this investment and see some results.

There are plenty of books on this subject on the market. Thanks again for choosing this one! Every effort was made to ensure it is full of as much useful information as possible. Please enjoy!

# Chapter 1: Why Rental Properties are the Best Investment Opportunity for You

You can go with many different investment options. Many people like to put their money in the stock market because many companies are investing in it, there are many different strategies they can use while others prefer mutual funds because of its simple yet flexible investment strategies, and it has less management cost. Some people like to start their own businesses and make a living from that. In addition, others will just put their money away in a retirement plan and hope that it is enough to get them by.

However, one of the best ways that you can invest your money is through real estate investing and there are few different methods you can use to do this. It is not easy being a landlord because of the risks involved, the obligations to fulfill, and the requirements that you need to comply. In addition, being a landlord has a lot of advantages: you will be able to receive a decent amount of money per month from the rental properties;you are financially secured as long as there is a tenant; and, since you are the boss, you get to decide on the terms and agreement and when to sell it. While others think that investing in the stock market is much better because the return of investment is superficial (stocks can often make up to 10% while real estate only rises about 3% a year), rental properties still have a lot of benefits. You don't have to start big in this kind of investment; you can start with one property.

Let's see why real estate investment is the best compared to some of the other forms of investment you can choose.

# Get Some Great Tax Breaks

There are reasons you would want to consider purchasing a rental property. The first benefit is that the government will offer you some great tax advantages when you do this so that they can get more investors to purchase a rental property, which then causes the supply of rental homes to increase.

You are considered a business owner or an investor under tax laws when you own a rental property. This is good news for you because it lets you make use of more tax deductions and much more benefits, compared to being an average homeowner. For example, you can deduct travelling expenses and property depreciation to help lower your annual taxes. There are many tax benefits available for someone investing in rental

3

properties, and talking with your accountant or financial advisor can ensure that you take advantage of all of them.

## Use the Money from the Bank to Fund This Investment

Another reason you should consider purchasing a rental property is you can use other people's money to help pay for it. This is leverage and it can help you to multiply the gains on your property value all at the same time.

Suppose you purchased a rental property for $100,000 and you put down 20% out of your own pocket and the 80% came from the bank. If the property value ends up rising to $110,000, you reaped a return of 50%! However, if you used your own money to fund that same property, then your returns are only 10%. 10% is still fine, but not as profitable as the 50%.

Most lenders will finance between 50-80% of the property price as long as you can come up with down payment and have a good credit history. In addition, finance companies are another place to look for a loan for a rental property.

## The Rental Property Can be Used as an Asset to Secure More Loans in the Future

At first, you may wonder why a rental property is considered an asset by a bank or another financial institute. It is important because once you have paid off a touch of the mortgage for your rental property; you can then use this as collateral.

What does this mean? You can pledge your rental property as an asset to get another loan if you need. This is helpful if you want to purchase another rental property down the road or if you want to start a new business later.

By paying off your monthly mortgage—through the rental payment of tenants—you can not only build up equity but also your personal credit scores. When you have a high credit score, you will have a higher chance of loan approval and lower interest rates next time that you want to take a loan out.

## Losses for Your Rental Properties Can Be Covered by Some Tax Relief

Besides all the tax deductions that we discussed earlier, investing in a rental property can also bring some tax relief if you end up with some losses. At first, some of your rental expenses may be high and they could exceed the rent you receive from your tenants. Expenses such as utility bills, repair costs, property insurance, and mortgage payment can easily take over your income at first. This can make it so that you make a loss in the beginning.

While these losses are not something that you want to see with an investment, the silver lining in all of these is rental losses can be used as a tax deduction against your other taxable income. Of course, this isn't the sole reason for you investing in a rental property, but it can help if it becomes tough for the first few years. As you pay off the mortgage and fix up the home, and as market values increase so you can raise rental payments, you will start to see a profit from this work.

## Values in Property Are Usually Less Volatile Than the Stock Market

Stocks can be a great investment, ones that can be bought and sold as quickly and as easily as you would like. This is good for someone who wants to try out the stock market, but then discovers it's not for them and they want out immediately. But because of this, stock prices can fluctuate much more than rental property values. In fact, a stock price can be so volatile that it could move up and down 5% or more in one day.

Real estate is more of a long-term investment. That is why the property market—while it goes up in most areas—is not that volatile. When you purchase a property to use as a rental investment, you don't plan to take it and sell it within a few weeks or even a few months. You plan to keep it for many years so you can pay down the mortgage and earn money. And most people who get into the market of real estate outside of flippers—who are rare and far between—plan to purchase a home and stick with it for a long time.

This can help keep the market for housing more stable. When you purchase a property, you won't have to worry about it going up or down in value in a short period of time. This means buying and selling a property can take more time. But this really stabilizes real estate prices, which can help shield your investment from overnight market crashes and other sell outs that happen in the stock market.

## Can Create a Passive Income for You

Your rental income can be more stable and frequent compared to some of the cash flow that you get from other investments. Your tenants–as long as you keep the property filled–will pay you the monthly rent, allowing you to have a stream of cash flow as long as you pay the monthly mortgage and taxes on the property on time.

Most rental property owners receive some rent from their tenants every month. However, if you're going with the stock market, your bonds would only pay you some interest every six months and stocks will only pay dividends every year, and that only happens if the company actually makes a profit.

Another reason rental properties may be the best option to go with is that if you hire a property manager to handle the day-to-day activities, then this becomes a hands-free affair and you are effectively earning a passive income from your work.

Rental properties have many benefits that you can enjoy. They take a touch of workin the beginning to get up and running, and they require maintenance and finding the right tenants. But if you can get all of these organized, you will quickly see that they are perfect for helping you get a steady cash flow; they can give you tax breaks and can even provide you with equity that can be used on future loans.

# Chapter 2: What Are Some of the Risks with Rental Properties?

Like any other type of investment, there are a lot of advantages when you own a rental property. However, there are also some risks involved when it comes to purchasing a rental property. You have to remember: this is a business endeavor and not just something fun to do on the side. A lot of money goes into rental properties— you are purchasing a whole house— and you have to be prepared for this new investment so you can make the most moneypossible. This chapter is going to focus on some of the risks that can come up with rental properties and some of the things you can do to limit these risks and get the best results.

# Buying a Property That Is in Worse Condition Than You Expected

The first thing you need to do when you get into this investment is pick the right property. You want the right location, the right price, and a property that won't take too long or won't cost too much to fix up. When you are looking for an investment property, you need to think of it as a business rather than a personal home that you will live in. You want a property that will make a good profit for you as soon as possible. You don't want to get reckless and overspend on the property before the first tenant walks in the door.

To help you avoid the risk of purchasing a new property that is in worse shape than expected, ensure that you get an inspection done. You need to bring an inspector to the property with you before purchasing. This takes up a few hours of your time, but these professionals will discover any problems or hidden damages that should be fixed before you rent out the property. They will also give you some ideas on spending budget to update the property before you purchase.

**Not Being Able to Get a Tenant for a Long Period of Time**

Another risk is not being able to get tenants. Once you purchase a good property and once it is ready to be rented out, you may run into trouble finding tenants. This is even riskier if you took a loan out from a bank to help purchase the property and you expected to get some rent each month to cover those payments. If you end up not being able to find the right tenant, you should cover up the mortgage, the property taxes, the insurance, and other expenses from your own salary or savings.

Look for tenants immediately, even before you finish purchasing the property. This gives you some leeway time to find the right tenants and you will get them inthe right time when the property is ready. You don't want to choose the first tenants that come along because this can cost you more money than not having a one. By starting early, you give yourself some room to find the right people to rent from you.

You can reduce this risk by doing your research and choosing a good property to invest in. Choose a property that is in a high-demand location with high-occupancy rates.

The more in-demand your property is, the easier it is to get tenants.

## Having Bad Tenants

While finding some tenants to live in your rental properties is important so you can make money, there are times you can't be provided with a profit. This happens when you end up choosing a bad tenant. Having that kind of tenant and not evicting them can sometimes be even worse than the risk of not having anyone to start with. Yes, no tenant means no earning; but with that kind of tenant, they may not pay the rent, they may destroy the house, and they may end up costing you more time and money than not having one.

Each property can become damaged a bit simply from people living in it. But bad tenants take this to the next level and may destroy things. They may refuse to pay your rent for a few months, making your cash flow stop. You then have to file a notice to a local court, schedule the date, and show up there, empty out the property, and then do the repairs before you can get a new tenant. These evictions can be costly and take a long time. You are spending on the mortgage and other expenses without earning any profits in the process.

It is best if you can avoid this risk to start with. Have some high selection criteria before you pick a tenant. You can write out your tenant rules ahead of time. You don't want to discriminate against someone for their social status, religion, gender, or age because this can get you in legal trouble. But you can look at their credit score, some references, and their past rental history to help you make informed decisions. This may make it so you will have vacant periods, but you will be further ahead doing this than being more costly for having a bad tenant.

## The Expenses on the Property Are Higher Than You Anticipated

When you become a landlord, the potential costs will not end just because you purchased the property. These rental properties will require constant expenses. You have to pay the mortgage payment, taxes (often higher a primary home tax), insurance, maintenance (varies depending on the type of tenants you have), and more.

If you calculated the right way and priced the rent well, then income that you make from your tenants will cover these expenses. Hopefully, you can also earn a positive cash flow from what's left. That is your overall goal when you start investing in rental properties.

But at times, the expenses may end up being more than what was anticipated. Maybe a tenant comes and causes a mess throughout the house. Maybe something major breaks and you have to fix it. Or, the market could go down and you aren't able to charge as much rent as you need. Having a plan in place is very important before you even consider venturing this type of investment.

To avoid any risks of paying more for the rental property rather than making money off it, ensure you really do your homework before you become a landlord. Get a pen and some paper and do the math. Make the correct calculations before you purchase a property so you know how much it will cost and how much you will earn. Add another 5% to give yourself a bit of wiggle room. If you wouldn't get a positive cash flow from this, then you shouldn't purchase the property.

## The Real Estate Market Starts to Fall

In recent times, the real estate market has been growing. But while the trend is positive, there really isn't a guarantee that this kind of trend is going to continue. One risk that you may encounter first with rental property investing is the concentration of your assets. For the most part, when you own a rental property, this is a serious concentration of assets because you will spend a larger portion of your net worth–sometimes all of it–just to get the property.

As the landlord, the first property investment is not going to be diversified–you only have one property at this point. If the neighborhood, the city, or even the national economy starts to go down, you could end up losing a large portion of your investment when depreciation occurs.

One option that you can follow to help reduce this risk is to diversify your investment a bit. This is not easy as a beginner because purchasing rental properties is expensive. You aren't selling them and making a profit, so you don't have any money to purchase another. But you can pull your money together with other investors and start a residential investment company. This is basically a small business that buys, rents, and sells rental properties.

Rental properties are a great investment that can help you to earn a great deal of money, especially over a long-term period. The benefits far outweigh the possible risks, but it is still important to understand that there are some risks with this type of investment, just like with any other form of investing. You should be aware of these risks and learn how to avoid them to get the best return on your investment.

# Chapter 3: The Best People to Work with During Your Investment

When you venture into rental property investing, you will find that you are not able to do all the work alone. This will just make the work harder than it should be and you will probably give up and not earn. Having a good team behind you the whole time can really make the process go smoothly and can help to reduce some of the risks that you face.

The people you want in your team can vary depending on the work you want to put in and the kind of project you are working on. Your team may include a mentor, a real estate agent, a contractor, and a good loan officer. Let's take a look at each of these individuals and explore why they can be so important in making your investment successful.

## Your Family

Working as a rental property investor takes a lot of time and work. You have to learn the market and search around for the right property. You have to make a purchase of that property. You have to do the repairs on the property and find the right tenants to live there. Even when tenants are there, you have to spend time doing any repairs and collecting rent. The work of a landlord can be rewarding, but it takes up a lot of your time and will keep going, even after you purchase the property.

You will need the support of your family during this time. You may need them to help you out with some of the repairs. You may need them to vent to during tough situations. In some cases, your family may be the ones who loan you money to help with purchasing the property or repairing it. There is nothing better for your overall success than having your family to support you through this process.

## A Mentor

Getting into real estate can be difficult. There are many things that you have to focus on, including the market status, how much you are spending, and finding tenants to name a few. Learning all those stuff before you get into the market can be a great way to reduce your risks, but nothing beats real-life experience. Working with an experienced mentor, who is willing to talk it over and offer advice when needed, can be an invaluable asset to you.

There are lots of places you can look for a mentor. You can talk to someone who has done real estate flipping or rental properties. These individuals have personal experiences doing the work and they can really show you how the process gets done. Depending on who you work with, they may even let you come along on some of the work and see how the process works upfront.

If you can not make connections with anyone who invests in rental properties in your area, then you can talk to real estate agents, contractors, or other people who work with properties and they can give you some insight into how to do this type of investment.

## An Accountant

At first, you may decide that you don't want to work with an accountant. You want to just handle this on your own and not to deal with another person. But even when you are starting and especially further down the line, you may decide that it is worth your time to have an accountant on your side.

A good and reliable accountant can help you keep track of all the finances of your new business. They can help you figure out current rent prices, determine the right price for the home, and help you set up a budget. And, they will help you during tax time to ensure you get the most tax deductions possible. In the long run, your accountant can end up saving you money!

You can explore a few different accountants to see who suits best for your needs. You might consider hiring an experienced accountant who has handled real estate accounts. They can ensure that you are getting your taxes done correctly and they will answer your questions about rental properties.

## A Good Loan Officer

As a rental property investor, you will work your way into owning not just one property. And until you really start to build up your equity in your properties or you have enough cash flow to purchase the property outright, you will need a loan to help finance your purchases. You will find that it is easier for you to work with the same loan officer each time. They can answer your questions and they know your payment and credit history. They can even offer new loan products and more to you that will help you get the most out of your investment.

We will talk about your loan officer more in the next chapter, but you need to carefully consider who you want to work with. There are many options. Local banks and credit unions are often best for this kind of investment. They want to help their local economy grow and they often have the best rates. Check into what rates each company can offer, pose questions, and see what requirements that the financial institute needs to help you get a loan.

## A Real Estate Agent

As the buyer of a rental property, it is a good idea to work with a real estate agent. The buyer's agent is going to be paid through the seller, which means you can enjoy their services and they will be there for you without you having to spend anything out of your own budget.

A real estate agent can be a valuable resource because they know the area really well. They have some great connections and can find some of the properties for you. Using the MLS and their contacts, you may even be able to hear about properties coming up on the market before anyone else does.

Your agent can be useful during the purchasing as well: they will do the paperwork for you; negotiate for the best price; help you get the inspections done; a good resource for finding workers that you need to do any major or minor fixes in the house. In some cases, they may even be able to recommend some potential tenants to help you get the renting started.

You can certainly choose to purchase a home on your own, but since the agent can provide you with a lot of resources and the seller is the one paying them, it is worth your time to find an agent to work with, at least in the beginning. If you are a beginner and don't know the market well and you don't want to deal with all of the paperwork, then hiring a real estate agent can make a big difference.

## A General Contractor

It is a good idea to have a general contractor that you can call when looking at a rental property, even after purchasing. To get the best price on a rental property, you should get a home that needs a little work. If it is brand new or in amazing shape, you are going to find the price is too high for your budget and you won't earn in the process.

Since you are going to work with some fixer-uppers in the process, you will need to work with a general contractor. They can take some time to look through the home before you purchase and help you know whether there are any major or minor fixes that need to be done and how much will be the cost. This can make a difference in whether you actually purchase the property or not, and can save you from some big surprises down the line.

Once you purchase the property, you can also use the general contractor to help you make some of the fixes. With some of the minor jobs, you can do them. But if you don't have the time, or if it is a major job that needs a professional, the contractor can do the work for you. A good general contractor will offer a good price, will complete the work quickly, and can work with you on any project.

Having the right team of professionals on your side can make the rental investment process easier. They can support you, help you keep track of all the finances, help you find a property, and even help you get the financing that you need to get you started. Take your time to find the right people to join your team and get the best results.

# Chapter 4: The Best Types of Rental Properties You Can Purchase and Make Money From

When you are ready to invest in rental properties, there are actually a few different options that you can choose from. Some are going to earn you more potential profits, but you should put in more work than others. Some will earn less profit in the beginning, but the tenants usually do a better job maintaining it and they will stay around. You have to balance the benefits and the risks of each option and decide which one is the best for you. Some of the different rental properties that you can choose from for your investment include:

## Apartments

The first option we are going to look at is apartments. These often include quite a few living arrangements in one building and can have a lot of potential for profits depending on how many rooms you can keep full with tenants. If you have 100 units in the building, there can be a large amount of profit with a reasonable rent. When renting these out, you should consider the rental charges, the allowed number of tenants in each unit, and whether or not you will take care of the utilities cost in the rent. You will be responsible for maintenance like mowing the grass and snow removal throughout the year.

However, there are some disadvantages. Yes, you can make a

lot of income, but keeping an apartment up and running can take a lot of work. And each of those tenants will have problems that they want you to fix. Apartments are also notoriously known for high turnover rates. Being able to keep all the units occupied at all times can be almost impossible and you may spend a lot of time advertising for and screening potential tenants to keep your income stream coming in throughout the year.

## Duplexes

Duplexes are the best of both worlds, combining the extra profits from apartments with some of the ease of a single-family home. These properties will usually have between two to eight separate living arrangements or apartments available, so you can open it up and split the mortgage payment between many people. You will have more work than you would find with a single-family home, but the potential income is much higher. Many tenants who go to duplexes are going to be around a lot longer than you find with an apartment, which can provide a good stream of income without having to search for new ones all the time.

Another benefit of these properties is that you can also live in one of them. If your property has eight living spots, you could rent out seven of them and let those tenants pay for the mortgage on their own. This gives you free living arrangements—the tenants pay for it for you—and you can just one call away if something happens that you need to take care of.

# Single-Family Homes

A lot of investors like to go with a single-family home to help them make an income from their property. These properties are easy to manage and often, the family that agrees to be your tenant will stay around for a couple years. They want to have stability and they don't like to move around for a long time. If you can get them in, you can have a steady income for a long time.

The downside to these types of properties is that they can only hold one family at a time so you won't be able to make a larger income like you can with apartments and duplexes. But most tenants who move into these homes will take good care of them and it will be less work on your side.

# Commercial Real Estate

You also have the option to rent out commercial real estate. This allows you to rent out office building, commercial spaces, or storefronts to interested businesses or companies. This takes more initial capital to get started, but it can definitely be worth it to make a large income.

There are many different types of properties that can fit here: you could own a single store or a strip mall and rent out to a lot of different tenants. If you own a spacious warehouse, you may rent it out to a company. You have to decide what kind of risk and investment you want to start with and which one works with your investing style.

There are some benefits to working with this. First, you can charge a higher rent so the potential for profit is higher. And, most businesses are interested in staying around for a long time because this provides more stability to their customers. This can provide you with a really steady income for three or more years. You may want to consider offering them a discount on the rent if they agree to stay for a longer period of time.

There are some disadvantages to this kind of investment as well, though. This investment type charges more upfront costs than some of the other options. This can make it harder to get into when you are starting and you may have to wait until you can save up more money to make it happen. Also, if one of your tenants or businesses ends up moving out, it can be hard to find someone to replace them and you would have to handle the mortgage and other expenses on your own.

These are just a few of the different properties that you will need to consider when you want to get into this kind of investing. There are some benefits and risks to each one, so you need to consider each of them and see which one seems the best for you.

# Chapter 5: Getting the Right Financing to Start Your Business and Help It Grow

When you are looking for a property to use as an investment, you also need to consider how you will finance it. It is unlikely that you will already have enough money to pay for it out of the pocket, so you will need to find some other methods to do it. Here, we are going to explore the available options that can help you finance the rental property so you can purchase it and start making money.

## Get a Conventional Loan from the Bank

Most rental property investors choose to go with a conventional bank loan. These often have the best terms and offer the most security when it comes to financing your investment property. If you own a residence, then you already have an idea of how to work with conventional financing.

A conventional mortgage conforms to the guidelines that Freddie Mac and Fannie Mae set up. And unlike some of the other loan options, like a USDA, VA, or FHA loan, it is not backed up by the federal government. With this conventional mortgage, you will need to put a 20% down payment on the home. Since this is more of an investment than a personal purchase, you may need to provide up to 30% for the down payment. You could use gifted funds to help pay this down payment, but you must make sure you document it properly before getting the mortgage.

When you work with a conventional loan, your personal credit score and history will be used to help determine if you will get approved and what interest rate you will get on the mortgage. These lenders are also going to take a look at your assets and income and the borrowers should be able to afford their current bills as well as the loan payments on the new property. Even if you plan to have a rent covering the rental property, you should be able to pay these out of pocket if things don't go well.

## Do a Hard Money Loan

One option that you should go with is a hard money loan. These loans can work for some investors because they are short-term loans that are not given out by a bank. Sure, you want to keep the property for long-term and may not be able to make the large payments for a long time and make a profit. But if you find that getting conventional funding is just not working for you, this option can help build up your credit score and you can get a conventional mortgage down the road.

This kind of loan can be useful because it looks more at the value of the property you want to purchase rather than on your personal credit. A good investor may go with this loan and while it works best with a property flip, it can help you get started.

When you know exactly what you want to get with your property, you can add in some higher than average loan costs to this formula. But make sure that you will not get into a lot of debt when you use this. This is riskier because the payments each month will be much larger. You want to go with a hard money loan, one that is beneficial to you and doesn't have too high of payments, and one that you will be able to convert over to a conventional loan later on to save you money.

Working with a hard money loan can be really expensive and you need to factor these expenses into your profitability calculations. These lenders will charge a very high interest rate—usually at least 14%—and they can carry multiple points and have high closing costs. Points are going to be paid up-front with each point being about 1% of the loan amount. This can cost you more upfront, but it helps when you need a quick short-term loan to finance the investment.

# Do a Fix and Flip loan

While being a landlord has a lot of perks, there are times when it will be a headache for the investor. You may decide that flipping is a better option. it means re-selling the property in order to make a big lump sum of money in the process.

These loans are often a smaller term and can be easier to get compared to a full 30-year mortgage. You have to work hard to get the property up and running and ready to sell to make the most profit. You can make a lot of money from this, but you also have to consider that you aren't earning any equity in the property and you won't be able to enjoy a steady stream of income when you choose this option.

If you are having trouble getting a loan to help you with this project, it may be a good idea to consider a short-term loan. This can help you get some of the financing that you need and can build up your credit history in the process. The monthly payments will be larger, but after a bit, you may be able to switch down to a less expensive option and the amount of equity that you earn in the process will be higher.

## Find a Local Investor in the Area

If some of the other options for financing do not work for you, then you may look for an investor who would help you out. You can start by searching in your local community. This can be tricky, though, because individual investors want to find ways to protect themselves so that you can't just run off with their money. But they may be excited to get started with the investment and may provide you with better rates than other options.

Choosing this option can be a great way to earn the financing you need at good rates. Before you approach an investor, make sure that you have a plan in place to impress them. Show them your investment plans, answer their questions, and even show them the terms that you are interested in sharing with them if they invest their money with you.

## Owner Financing

You should also consider doing owner financing on the property. There are some owners who are willing to do this kind of financing. They find that it earns them extra on the sale of their home and opens up the market to more buyers than waiting for someone with a conventional mortgage. You can get what you want without going through a traditional bank, and the seller can make even more money on their house.

For this option–instead of working to get a conventional mortgage–you would instead make monthly payments to the person who owns the property now. You would have to come up with a down payment at the time that you close, but this is often less than 10%. The owner will be charged with the interest as well, setting it about 1 or 2 percentage points above the conventional mortgage rates, but sometimes they may consider setting it higher. When you are ready to resell the property, you will pay off the remainder of the loan balance and you can keep the profit.

Many investors will try to look for this kind of option if they want to purchase a property, but they can't come up with a good down payment to use traditional methods. The owner is just going to carry the mortgage for that property, using the method they did to purchase it. You would still pay for the repairs and take ownership of the property. The hardest part is often finding the right seller who would do this.

Another option similar to this is using an owner financing. This is when you purchase the property as "subject to" the ongoing mortgage. The buyer will pay the seller the amount between the purchase price and the balance left on the mortgage at that time. They then take over the payments of the seller's mortgage. However, you need to double-check before you decide to do this because some mortgage contracts say this is not allowable.

## Tap into Your Home Equity

Another option that you can work with is to draw on the equity in your personal residence. You can do this through a home equity loan or through a cash-out refinance. Depending on your mortgage and the rules in your area, you can borrow up to 80% of the equity value of your home towards purchasing a second home. If you have paid off quite a bit of your personal home and have some equity, this could be a great way to get the money that you need for this investment.

There are some benefits and risks in using this kind of financing, and often, it depends on the loan type that you go with. With a home equity loan, you are going to borrow against the equity of your home in a similar way that you would with a credit card. And for a specific amount of time, the payments would just be on the interest. The rate on this is variable, which means there is the potential it will go up if the prime rate rises.

You can also go with a cash-out refinance. This option has a fixed rate, but often it extends the life of the mortgage you already have. This longer term for the loan means that you pay more in interest over the life of the mortgage on the primary residence. You would need to weigh this against the expected returns that your investment property will bring in.

## Tips to Help You Get the Financing You Need for Your Investment

In addition to following some of the steps above, there are a few other things that you can do to increase your chances of getting the financing that your new investment needs. Some of the best tips that you can get financing include:

- *A good down payment*: Since your mortgage insurance isn't going to cover properties used for investing, you should put down a minimum of 20% to help secure the traditional financing that you want. If you can put down 25% or more down, you may be able to get an even better rate for your property. If you are looking at rental properties and you don't have the down payment, it may be time to look at other options. You can consider a second mortgage for that property, but that is difficult to get.

- *Being a borrower the banks like*: There are a lot of factors that come into play when the bank or other financial institution decides to give you a loan. One thing that you can do ahead of time is to check your credit score and see you can improve to make it better. If it is below 740, it will cost you more money to get the same interest rate on your score. Also, make sure that you have enough money in the bank to cover six months of living expenses because this can make you look more attractive to a bank.

- *Stay away from the big banks*: Big banks are all about the bottom line and if you have anything on your history that is less than stellar, they will either deny you the loan or charge outrageous rates so you have a hard time making a profit at all. Local banks and credit unions are much better options. They will take more diverse customers than the big banks and they want to see their local community grow. If you have any blemishes on your credit or you want to work with someone who is a bit easier, then working with a local financial institution can be better.

- *Considering owner financing*: This is hard to come by in some cases, but there are some times you may be able to get the owner to do the financing for you. You may have to convince the seller to do this for you because they don't want to keep the property and they don't want their credit score ruined in the process. You should come up with a contract and stick with the agreements to make this work.

- *Thinking creatively*: If you are looking at a good property and you think it will do well with investing, you may want to find some creative methods to get the down payment or even the money to do renovations. Using credit cards, insurance policies, or a home equity line of credit can help you out here. Be careful and weigh whether these options are good and if you can to pay them back. For example, credit cards contain high-interest rates so you should be careful in using them.

Financing an investment property can take some time. Lenders want to make sure that you have a good credit score; that you have a good plan behind your investment. They also want to make sure that you can afford your current bills and the new loan amount that you are asking for. Work with some of the tips above and you will find that it is easier than you think to get the funding that your investment property needs.

## Steps to Help You Get the Funding That You Want

When you are ready to get the financing, it is important to know the steps in order to get funding for your loan. The first step is to check out your credit score. All financial institutions are going to take a look at your credit score to make sure that you don't have too much debt, that you don't have any late payments, and that there is nothing else that they need to be concerned about when they give you a loan.

If you take a look at your credit score and notice that there is something that may concern them, or you see that your score is not high enough, then you should work on it before you try to reach out to a financial institution. Get some of your debts paid down, find out how you can close out some bad accounts, and learn other ways that you can put up with your credit score so you look more attractive to a lender.

Next, you need to write out a business plan to show to the financial institution. This is not just a loan for your personal home. It is to help you start out a new investment and a new business. This means you need to treat it that way. The financial institution who becomes your lender will also want to see that you have a plan in place and that you have an entry strategy, a reasonable timeline, enough money to pay off the mortgage while you wait for a tenant, and that you have a good exit strategy in place.

Take the time to write this business plan out and make it look professional and well-thought-out. You can find some templates to help with this so you can really impress the lender. You should show this to every lender you want to work with, so keep a few extra copies on hand to make it easier when you need to talk to a new lender.

You should also have a down payment. This is a loan for an investment so you are not going to get some of the other options such as no down payment like you can with a personal home loan. You should come up with some form of down payment, and the larger this payment can be, the better off you will be. You can discuss the best amount with your lender. A larger amount will not only give you more equity in the property but can also save you a lot of money since you can get a lower interest rate.

You may need to show some other information as well. If you have ever purchased a home for your personal use, then you know a lot of what the lender is going to look for. You need your pay stubs and that of anyone who is going to be on the loan with you such as your spouse or a partner, information about any debts, and more. If the bank asks for anything else, make sure to get this information to them as quickly as possible. This can help speed up the process and will get your loan money in your pocket as quickly as possible.

Make sure that you take the time to shop around. Even local banks in the same town can offer you different rates and benefits for working with them. If you shop around and compare the rates and offers from several banks–at least two or three– you will ensure that you are getting the best deal and won't have to pay any more on the loan than necessary.

After you have presented this information to a few lenders, you should start to get some offers, as long as all the information is in place. Then you can compare the offers that you get and pick the one that will help cover the loan at the lowest rates. The lower rate is going to make a difference in how much you are going to spend over the life of the loan, as well as how much the payment will be every month. Carefully look over each one to make sure you get the best deal possible when you sign.

# Chapter 6: What Makes a Good Rental Property?

Now that you have some ideas of where to get your financing and you are now ready to start searching around, you may wonder what is going to make a good property to help you get started with investing in rental properties. There are several different factors to help you analyze all of the properties that you look for. It is best to consider each of them to ensure you are getting the best property that will earn the most money. Some of the things that you should consider when picking out a good rental property to invest in will include the following:

# The Neighborhood

The quality of the neighborhood you purchase in is going to influence your vacancy rate and the tenants you will get. For example, if you purchase a property that is near a college, your tenants will be mostly students, and you will have vacancies on a regular basis such as during the summer breaks and when a semester ends.

Knowing your target market can really make it easier for you to pick out the right neighborhood. You can think about what your perfect tenant is looking for when they rent, and then look in that neighborhood so you can provide it to them. Each type of tenant prefers a different area. For example, a family will want an area near the schools and parks and with other children but an older couple may want to be somewhere quieter.

In addition, check out the rules in some neighborhoods. There are some municipalities that don't want to see the homes turned into rentals so they will put up a lot of red tapes and high permit fees to help discourage this kind of investing.

## How Much the Property Costs

When looking at properties, you need to consider how much it costs. You don't want to go for an expensive property. If so, the mortgage, insurance, and taxes are going to be too much and you won't be able to charge enough in rent to cover all of it.

You always have to look for properties that are lower in price but won't need a lot of money on the renovations. Before purchasing the property, you should get a calculator and figure out the numbers. Look at how much the mortgage will be and how high the interest is. Look at how much you will spend each month on any repairs, the taxes, insurance, and everything else you owe on the property. Also, include a little bit so you can earn a profit.

Take that number and compare it to the average rent in your area. If it is at or under this number, then the property is perfect for you and you should consider putting in a bid. If the amount ends up being lower than the average rent, you can raise it and make an even larger profit in the process. Never invest in a property without running all the numbers ahead of time.

## How Much Work Needs to Be Done

You also need to consider how much work the property needs to have done. If you purchase a property for a good price, but then you have to completely remodel it, this is going to take more time and money than you can afford. You should spend a little bit on renovations when it comes to purchasing a rental property, you don't want to spend too much of your budget on this part.

As you look through properties, take notes and some pictures. You can even consider bringing a contractor along with you to look over the property. This gives you a good idea of how much work you should do, and then you can get estimates on how much it will cost. If you can purchase the property and fix it up while still making a profit on the rent you would charge, then this property is a good one to invest in.

## Property Taxes

The next thing that you need to take a look at when checking out a property is its taxes. You will quickly find that when you look at a town, the property taxes are not the same in all areas. If the area is newer—if you are near schools and if you are closer to the country—you may pay a different property tax than anyone else. You need to know exactly the property taxes that will be charged to you.

You need to know the exact amount of property taxes ahead of time. If you wait until after the property is yours, you may be in for a bit of sticker shock. Don't try to come up with an estimate on this either. Some investors will look at other similar properties and try to guess their property taxes. But each property is different and depending on its size, where it is located, how big and more, the property taxes may be different than other similar properties. Visit the country assessor in your area to get an accurate number for this one.

# Schools

If you are purchasing a home big enough for a family, then you also need to take a look at some of the local educational facilities nearby. If a property is good but the schools are not close by, then it is going to greatly affect the value of your investment. While you have some concerns about the cash flow you will get each month, the overall value of the rental property is going to come into play when you sell it, and having a property near schools can make a big difference.

If you are in a market that has several options for schools, consider which the best is. You should need to pick out a property that is near a private school to help attract those properties. Or if you know one of the schools doesn't do well with state testing, you should need to avoid that one when you pick out your property.

## Crime Rate

No one wants to move somewhere that has a lot of criminal activity or a high crime rate. Even when they are renting rather than buying, they want to make sure they live in a place that is safe and secure for them and their families. You can choose at your local library or check with the police in order to see the crime statistics in all the neighborhoods near you. Some of the concerns that you need to pay particular attention to include vandalism, petty crimes, serious crimes, and how recent the activity of crime is. You can also ask how frequently the police get called to the area to help see if it is a safe option for you to invest in and if your tenants will like it.

If you are uncertain about how the crime rate is in one area, make sure to find out. You can talk to the local police to help you with this. They can answer all your questions and will give you more information than you can find from anywhere else. You can also make an inquiry around town to see if there are any areas that might be noisy or might have other issues that you should be aware of before making a purchase.

## Job Market

You need to look at the employment rates in the area you are considering purchasing. If the job market is poor, then it is hard to find tenants who can pay higher rates. You should find a location that has growing employment opportunities because these are going to attract more people to the area, which means that you have more potential tenants.

To help you figure out the employment rates in a particular area, just head to the local library or to the U.S. Bureau of Labor Statistics. If you notice in the newspaper that there is a new company moving to your area or nearby, then this may be a good place to invest in before all the workers flock to the area.

Now, it is possible that the housing prices are not going to move the way that you want. For example, the housing prices are going to react, either in a positive or a negative way, depending on the company moving in. The fallback point here is that if you want to move to the town that has this company, then your renters will like this area as well. If they wouldn't be happy with that company, you probably shouldn't invest here.

# Amenities

Take the time to check out the potential neighborhood for current or projected public transport hubs, theaters, gyms, hospitals, malls, parks, and other perks that renters might be interested in. Cities–and even specific parts of a city–have a lot of promotional literature that can inform what public amenities are available. You can then look at an area that has a lot of amenities and see if there are some reasonable properties that will meet your needs for a rental investment property.

The amenities that are the most important will vary depending on what kind of tenant you are looking to work with. If you are interested in working with college kids, you will want to have the college nearby or some local restaurants and night spots. If you are catering to single professionals, you want to make sure you are near the business district. If you are catering to families, then you want to make sure that parks, schools, and other family-friendly activities are nearby.

## Future Development in That Area

You also need to take a look at whether or not there will be any future developments in that area. The municipal planning department can provide you with all the information you need about the new developments that will happen in thearea or even any that is currently zoned in that area.

If you look through this information and you notice there are new business parks, malls, and apartment buildings going up in this area, this is a good thing because it shows this is a good growth area. While this growth can be important, you need to watch out for it a little bit. Sometimes a new development could harm the price of the properties nearby, such as when they cause the loss of activity-friendly green space in a family-friendly area. This additional new housing may also provide some competition for your property, which can make it harder to get tenants.

## Number of Vacancies and Listings in That Area

If you are looking through the market and you notice that one area or neighborhood has a very large number of listings, then this is something that you can look into. You may see that it is a seasonal cycle and will end soon, or it is a sign that the neighborhood has gone bad. As an investor, you need to figure out which is happening before you purchase. If the neighborhood has gone bad, it is probably not a good idea for you to purchase a home there because you will not find any tenants.

Similar to the idea of listing, the vacancy rates in a particular neighborhood will help you know whether you will have success in attracting tenants. A high rate in vacancies means that you should have lower than average rents in order to attract tenants. Low vacancies can be good for you as a landlord because it means you can raise the rental rates.

## How High the Rent Is

When you purchase this type of investment, you are planning on earning money from the rent that your tenants pay. You need to know the average rent in the area so you can base your own rental prices from the property you want to purchase. If you look at the average rent and find that you can't be able to cover the mortgage, taxes, insurance, and repairs of a property, then you should keep looking. You should never go into the investment assuming that you can charge way more than the average price for a property because tenants will not agree to rent from you.

You can research the area well enough so you can also gauge where the rents will go in the next five years. If you can afford the area at this time, but you find that there are some big improvements that need to be done and the property taxes will soon increase, the amount you spend may get too high and you won't be able to afford it later.

Basically, you need to do the math and if you can get the property and pay all the expenses while making a bit of an income while staying at market rent prices, then this is a good investment. If you are worried about doing this, then you should consider a different property to help you earn an income.

**if you are finding this book useful in any way, a review on Amazon is always appreciated!**

Always overestimate rather than underestimate when it comes to this. You don't want to purchase the property, fix it up, and then search for some tenants just to find out that you are not able to charge the amount of rent you wanted for that property. It is always best to add another 5 to 10% to your costs to make sure you get everything covered.

## Natural Disasters

Preparedness is the key during a natural disaster. You will never know when an earthquake, tornado, or hurricane will strike or a flood will rise in your area, whether it is located in a high-risk zone or not.

As a landlord, you should pay attention to the structural details of the property you want to put your money into. It is very important to run a check on the roof, walls, and most especially all the building's foundation. For old buildingsor houses, wear and tearare normal so you need to make sure that it has been reinforced. Before you purchase a property, ensure that, as much as possible, it is at its excellent condition.

You also need to secure an insurance when purchasing a rental property. You need to have a sufficient insurance coverage for the building structure and its contents; you need to also have a firm idea on how much you will spend for insurance on your property so you can factor this into your costs. If you are purchasing a property located in an area prone to tornadoes,hurricanes, flooding, earthquakes, and other natural disasters, you are going to pay extra for this insurance coverage. This can really cut into your profits if you are not cautious. You must do these calculations ahead of time so better if you talk to an insurance provider and seek for the policies they offerand what rates are for the area you want to purchase in.

Choosing the right rental property can make all the difference when it comes to how successful you are. If you pick out a property that is slightly worn out or you have to pay a lot extra in insurance, it could eat away at your profits and can even make it hard to find the right tenants.

# Chapter 7: How Do I Purchase My First Property for This Type of Investment

At this point, it is time to start looking at the steps you should take in order to find the first property and then purchase it. This is actually a longer process. It is not as simple as running out and purchasing the first property that gets on the market. When you put money into a property, remember these things: be well-informed about this type of investment and create a winning mindset.

You need to fully understand the market you are working with, get the right financing, find tenants, make an offer, fix up the home, and collect rent money in the process. All of these come together to help you become a good landlord.

Let's take a look at some of the steps that you need to follow in order to purchase your first rental property.

## Do Your Research Fully Before Chasing the Property

It is easy as a new investor to jump directly into this and purchase the first property that you find. But you need to do your research before you enter the market. As soon as you decide that rental investing is the right decision for you, you need to do your homework, researching, and learning as much about the market as you can. Some of the questions that you may want to consider to help you with your research include researching:

- What type of property do you want to purchase for this investment?

- How much can you afford and are comfortable with paying?

- What kind of neighborhood are you interested in purchasing and investing in?

- What is the average rent in that area and can you work with that to earn money?

- What is the return on investment you are hoping to make and is that reasonable for that area?

As a beginner, you may find that doing your research can be hard, mainly because you are not yet sure what kind of questions you should ask. Think about this as a new business, because that is what an investment is, and think about all the questions that you should ask before making this important decision.

## Decide Who Your Target Market Is

One thing you should consider when you are ready to look for some investment properties is your target market. This may seem somewhat silly, but it can actually really influence the properties you pick and the way that you conduct your business.

Are you looking for a single-family home that a family will move in and stay in for a few years? Then you should consider a nice family home that has three or four bedrooms near the schools, near some parks, near some malls, and where other families with children live. If you want to cater to the older generation, you would want to look for properties that are in safe parts of town, properties that are single level, and ones that won't have many repairs for the tenant to deal with. If you want to deal with an apartment, you will have to consider whether you want to rent to families, singles, or college kids to determine where you will purchase and how big each unit is.

Knowing what market you want to cater to can really help you think about the type of property you want to pick out. You never want to just pick the first property that comes up. It may require too much work, or it may not work for the kinds of renters in your area. Writing out this criteria ahead of time can help you prepare and will make it easier to find a property that will market itself to your target market.

## Set up Your Plan and Pick Your Criteria

After you have spent some time looking at the market and learning everything you can about prices, rent averages, and what new things may come into the area, it is time to make out your personal plan and set your criteria. You should spend time writing out the plan and the goals so you can refer back to them and keep yourself on track when you start looking at properties.

When you are looking for a property and have decided that you can afford a home between $100,000 and $150,000, it can be easy to fall in love with a house that is $175,000; but that may be above your budget and you won't be able to afford it and make your mortgage payment. When you lay out your plans, you will do a better job holding yourself accountable through this process.

One thing that you may want to do before you even go and look at a property is to write out the criteria and take this paper with you. It is easy to see a property and think it is fine to change your rules or move a little bit off course. But soon, you get a lot of off courses and you get a property that is way too expensive, one that won't match with your current market, or one that will need too many fixes before you can even rent it out.

# Arrange the Financing

Before you can put in an offer on a property, you need to figure out your financing. No seller will accept your offer if they don't have a pre-approval for the amount of the property. It can save a lot of time and will help you to know how much you can spend before you even take a look at the available properties for investing.

So, when you are ready to start looking for properties, make sure you talk about this with the bank. They will be able to give you an idea of how much you can buy and they can discuss the different financing options that you can use before you make your choice.

Remember, there are many places you can shop around with in order to find a good loan that will help you out. You need to find the right financial institution that will help you out. But they aren't just going to hand you the money and let you do what you want with it. They expect you to step forward and show that you are responsible, that you can handle the new business, and that you are not going to lose all their money.

This is why there are often some strict guidelines in place. You need a good credit score before you even start asking the bank to finance you. If you have any blemishes on the credit score, consider fixing those ahead of time so you can present a clean slate to the bank. You should have some kind of down payment since this is an investment rather than a personal property. Even some of the down payment can really help. And the bank will require that you have enough personal income to pay back the loan with your current income for that time when the loan is due before a tenant and in between tenants.

In addition to the things above, you need a few things. Some banks will require that you have a business plan to show how you plan to use the money, your expected timeline on the project, and when you plan to start earning money back. Take your time here because this really shows the bank how serious you are about this investment. A good business plan will make or break your bid for a loan.

You can consider looking at several different places to get your funding. Different banks can offer you different interest rates, different terms, and even different options when it comes to your loans. Even banks in the same area are going to show some differences. Shopping around a bit can help you get the best deal when it comes to your financing.

## Begin Shopping Around for Some Properties

And now, the exciting part! You are going to start looking through your area to find a property that would be perfect as a rental property. You may have to take some time here and really search. But having patience will really pay off when you get into real estate because you will get the best deals.

You should start by looking on the MLS to see what properties are listed. This will provide you with the information you need on a lot of homes in your market. Even better, consider working with a real estate agent. They know the market and they can really help you through every step of the process. In this step, they are going to get you in touch with the information you need to really know which properties are best.

## Make an Offer When You Find a Property

When you find the property and you have already checked it out, it is time to make an offer on the property. Your real estate agent, if you are working with one, is going to fill out the paperwork based on your request and then will submit that offer to your selling agent. Then the seller's agent will bring that offer to the seller and negotiations are going to begin from there.

You want to make sure that during negotiations, you only offer the amount that makes the most sense for you. You should offer less so that you have some room to negotiate with the seller. Before sending out an offer, be willing to walk away from the deal if it doesn't go the way that you want. This helps you to keep the emotions out and gives you the upper hand so you don't spend too much on the property.

During this time, remember that you are not only negotiating the price with the seller. Depending on how strong the deal is and how popular that property is, there are some other things you need to add into the offer for the seller to consider including:

- Inspection contingency
- Closing date
- Seller financial concessions

- Financing contingency

These are important items and can help you get things done and then walk away if there are more issues with the house than you knew about. Once you sign the agreement with the seller and all the terms are agreed upon, you can then move on to get the stuff done before your closing date.

## Do Your Due Diligence

You and your seller have agreed on a price and the closing date is ready. Now you need to go through and do your due diligence. During this period, you need to spend the money on an inspector who can look over the property. They can let you know the condition of the house and if any of those defects are going to cost you money later on. If there is a major issue with the house, you have the option to go back and re-negotiate with the seller.

Now, you don't want to nickel and dime the seller if you are in a hot market. They can refuse to do the work and walk away from the deal. But it is fine to ask for some major problems with the home to be fixed. You can discuss things with your real estate agent to determine if the fix is something you should push for or not before purchasing.

This is also the time when you will finalize all the financial agreements with your lender. The title company will take over to help get the transaction taken care of and to ensure all the right papers get put in your day. When your closing date comes, you should sign documents before getting the keys to this property to take care of as your own.

# Fix up the Property

In most instances, you should do some work to the property. The right price for a property is not going to show up unless you put in the work as well. Sometimes the work will be simple, like a new paint job and replacing a few appliances. Other times the property is going to need more work. Either way, you should have factored the cost for these improvements into your budget so there should be no surprises there.

As soon as you purchase the property, it is time to get the work done on it. You want to get the work started and completed as soon as possible. If it takes you six months to get the property ready for someone to live in, that means you have to come up with the mortgage payment for 6 months without any rental money coming in.

Move quickly so that you can get your tenants in there and start earning money.

## Find Your Tenants

After you find the property and you have fixed it up, it is time to find your tenants. You will never make any money on the property and will be responsible for the mortgage if you don't find any tenants to live in there. Some landlords start advertising the vacancy before the property is completely ready in the hopes of having someone ready to move in as soon as possible.

Tenants may be plentiful, but there are times when they will be hard to come by. It often depends on the area, the time of year, and more. Advertising early on can make it easier for you to find your target tenant as early as possible so you can start making money.

When you are looking for a tenant to live in your property, you should be very selective. A good tenant is going to stay in your property for a long time, providing you with a steady stream of income. You should have them fill out an application and provide a rental history and references to ensure that they will be reliable and won't cause more problems than it is worth.

## Enjoy the Profits from Your Work

When you get to this point, congratulations! Your property is filled and you are going to earn money from your monthly rent. This may be a little bit slow in the beginning because you are paying off the mortgage and all the other expenses. But as you pay things off and potentially raise the rent as values appreciate in the future, you will start to earn more and more income. You can then decide whether you want to take on another rental property and grow your business and investment even more.

# Chapter 8: I'm Low on Finances, How do I Get Started Quickly?

Some people worry about being able to start with a rental property. They are not able to come up with tens of thousands of dollars in order to put in a down payment, and they worry they will never be able to get into the market. The good news is that there are a few options that you can use in order to get into this market without having a lot of money. Some of the options that you have available when you are low on finances include:

# Investing Without Using a Down Payment

When purchasing a property, it is sometimes hard to come up with a 20% or larger down payment. You may be low on funds, but still dream about investing in the real estate market. There are some options you can work with that will help you to invest, even if you only have a small down payment or no down payment at all.

First, you can consider working with seller financing. If you have a motivated seller, they may be willing to give you the loan for the property. You could offer to give them some higher monthly payments that can work as your down payment. You could negotiate a deal with the seller where they pay the down payment to the lender to help sell the property faster. They may expect you to pay them back, or they could do it as a way to lower the price for you. No matter which method you go with, you should write up an agreement with a real estate attorney to make sure you and the seller are protected from anything turning out badly in the agreement.

Another option is to lease the property with the option to buy later. You can slowly invest in the rental property by making payments on a lease agreement until you come up with enough money to buy. At least a few your payments would be credited to your purchase price. If you go with this option, make sure that the agreement states the final price rather than having it as an assumption.

Define the exact amount of the rental payment that should go to the final purchase price so you are protected.

Working out a trade can be an option as well. This one is not as common since most buyers need to pay off the mortgage when they sell their house so they won't want to barter anything. But if you do this one, you would barter some other property you have or a specialized skill. You could offer furniture, artwork, appliances, and more to get the property.

And finally, you could decide to take over the mortgage payments for the other party. If you want to invest in some real estate but you aren't able to afford the down payment, you can offer to take on the mortgage payments in exchange for the deed. You need to look at the existing loan of the seller because some loans don't allow this kind of thing to happen.

There is a variation of this last one where you agree to take over some of the other debts of the seller such as their credit card payments, instead of doing a down payment. Put this all in writing because the seller may be nervous about doing this. You could easily not pay the amount on the credit cards and then the seller has the debt and a bad credit score with no way to get the house back.

## Co-Investing with Someone Else for a Down Payment

Sometimes, you may need to work with someone else to get your properties. This can cut a bit into your profits, but when you share the work and share the expenses, it takes out some of the risks. The first thing you can do here is to bring in a partner. Both of you can pool together your money and then take on the expenses, the work, and the profits from that property. Make sure that the two of you write out a contract that is going to establish who is responsible for what, and how you plan to divide up the profits.

If you are stuck with who to invest with, consider doing it with a building contractor. This can be really helpful if you plan to do electrical, plumbing, and carpentry in the property and you don't have the right skills to do it on your own. Then you can take the profits that you make on that sale, share the agreed upon amount with the contractor and then save for your next property.

## Borrowing Money to Get Your Down Payment

In some cases, you may decide that it is best to borrow money from friends or family. This is definitely a place where you are going to need to write out an official promissory note that has some due dates for the payments. You can include the interest rates that the other person will charge and whether or not they have any ownership in the property. You have to consider the relationship with the person you are asking money from. It is possible the rental property will be a failure and if you can't pay the money back like agreed, can this harm relationship? You have to consider whether the real estate venture is worth ruining your relationship with someone who is close to you.

You can also consider using a home equity loan to help you get started. We spent some time discussing this before, but this is an option for those who are low on start-up costs with your investment. These loans are not going to cost you any down payments and sometimes can offer you a lower interest rate than others.

This option is will allow you to take out a loan for the down payment on your project on top of the mortgage that you have on your personal residents. This is sometimes a second mortgage and other times it is a line of credit. You want to make sure that you can pay off this amount because you could risk losing your own home if you can't.

And finally, consider a microlender. These types of loans often go by the name of peer to peer lending and they will help a borrower find a relatively small loan. These loans are often going to be less than $35,000. You need to do some research on these and learn about the regulations and rules so you don't run into any misunderstandings about how they work later on in the process.

# Chapter 9: Repairing and Maintaining Your Rental Properties

Once you have purchased your new property, it is time to get to work. There is likely to be a few things that you need to take care of in the property to make sure it is ready for the tenants to move into. If you did well with the seller, there shouldn't be anything major to work on at this point, so that is the good news here. But you are now in charge of this property. But once you buy a home or property, it is a continuous process of repair and maintenance. You have to clean up the property, conduct preventive maintenance, fix exterior and interior issues and damages, make sure all essential services are working (water, electricity, plumbing, heating, provided appliances and equipment), and ensure that everything works properly the whole time you own it—even if a tenant is living there.

The first thing is to do any renovations and updates. You may decide to add in a room, take down some walls to open it up, do some painting, do some landscaping, or anything else that you can to increase the value of the property. The more you can do for a low price, the better. This helps you attract more tenants and can allow you to ask for a higher rent.

In addition to these renovations to improve the value of the home, there are a few other things that you can do to help with routine property inspections and repairs of the property, whether you are preparing it before a tenant moves in or afterward:

- Keep the wood exterior on the home painted. This can lead to some softness and even deterioration of the wood if you don't keep up on this, and this repair can be really costly to work with.

- Check the dirt around your foundation. It should be sloping away from the foundation. If you see there are some holes around it, fill them and then add dirt backfill around it to help the water drain away, rather than inside and into the home.

- Check the gutters, especially in the fall. You want to keep these free of debris and leaves. Failing to do this can really let water back up into the gutters. The overflow from this could lead to water getting into the home and causing damage there. You can also add in some extenders to the downspouts so they are not able to empty to the foundation.

- Take some time to check the doors and windows for any gaps. Use some weatherproof sealant to help prevent water from getting into the home. These areas should be sealed up to make sure that water can't get in and cause damage. It is also a good way to keep the utility costs down because heat won't be able to get out.

- Take the time to inspect the trees on the property. Look for dead limbs or any that are hanging low and need some work. Look at the base of the tree. If you see that there is some rot on the bottom, they need to be cut down to avoid them falling onto your property.

- Check the roof occasionally. You want to see if there are any missing or damaged shingles. After some high winds or bad storms, be especially vigilant. These bad shingles can end up allowing water to get into the home, which can damage the property and cause mold to grow. Fixing these issues with drywall and mold cleaning can be very expensive,so stay on top of it before problems arise.

- If your property has a fireplace that burns wood, you should make sure that the chimney has an inspection and is cleaned out once a year. If you don't, it can cause a chimney fire. Make sure to give your tenants plenty of time to prepare for the cleaning to be done.

- To keep the property safe, you should clean out and inspect the heating and air conditioning systems at least one time a year. And each month, the filters should be changed. This ensures that the system will run in a more efficient manner and there won't be as much wear and tear.

- If your property does have a crawl space, then you or a professional needs to get into this area at least one time a year to check it out. Look along the plumbing and walls to see if there are signs of leaking. If you smell a musty smell, puddles on the floor of the crawl space, or water bills that are high, then there could be a problem. If you see that this area has some standing water, do not go in because illegal wiring could be there and you will get electrocuted. Call a professional contractor to help you get rid of that water and find out what is going on there.

- If your circuit interrupters have a problem, you need to test or trip them each month to make sure that they will function the way that you want. Failure to do this on a regular basis could result in the ground fault circuit interrupters that are not going to reset or not trip. You can either do this on your own or teach the tenants how to do it if they don't want you to come over all the time.

- Fix anything that goes wrong. Once the tenant moves into the home, you need to be prepared to take on the work if something stops working the proper way. Things are going to break or need to be fixed, and this becomes a bigger issue the longer you have the home. It is up to you to get it fixed, or hire someone else to fix it, within a reasonable amount of time after the tenant lets you know about it. If the issue at hand is going to cause harm and is an emergency to the tenant, you need to get over there to fix it right away.

In many cases, the tenant is going to be responsible for some things on the property, such as mowing and snow removal, unless this has been discussed ahead of time and is in the lease. The tenant is also expected not to do any damage, beyond normal wear and tear, on the property.

If you fail to do the right maintenance or fix things when they break in the property, the tenant can withhold your rental payments and may be able to file charges against you. They have the right to void the lease and leave as well. If the tenant doesn't keep the home in good shape and pay their rent, you have some options in place as well.

# Chapter 10: Tips for Working with Your Tenants

Once you have purchased a property to work with, you need to get tenants into the building. Without tenants, you will not earn any money and all the responsibility of paying for the mortgage and the other fees on the property will fall to you. The sooner you can get the tenant into the building and paying rent, the better off you will be in terms of getting a good return on your investment.

Getting tenants can be a challenge sometimes. You have to advertise for the tenant, and then when you get some interested parties, you have to do some screenings to ensure they are a good tenant and will stay with you while paying rent on time. It is important to take your time through this process because a bad tenant can be much worse than no tenant at all. Some of the steps that you need to do when selecting your own tenants include:

## Advertising for Tenants

As soon as you own the property, consider listing it as a rental property. Going through all the steps that we will talk about in this chapter can take some time; and the earlier that you can get started, the earlier you can get that tenant in there and start making money. You can easily look through applications and do the screenings while you finish up any work on the property.

There are different methods that you can use to advertise your listing. You can start with your local newspaper.

You can put a sign in front of the property to let those driving by know about the vacancy. You can use social media; make connections, use sites like Zillow, and more.

One of the best methods is with the word of mouth. You can enlist the help of your real estate agent and friends to help spread the word. This often works better than some of the other methods and can often provide you with better tenants than the other options as well.

## Choosing the Best Tenants

As a landlord, you will quickly learn that there are good and bad tenants. While there is no screening method that will always guarantee you won't get a bad tenant—and many landlords who have been in the business a long time can tell you stories about that

one bad tenant they will never forget—
there are some factors that you need
to pay attention to when you want to
find a great tenant for the rental. Here
are some of the things you should pay
attention to when choosing a tenant.

*Follow the Law*
The first step here is to follow all the
laws. A landlord must treat all of their
prospective tenants in an equal
manner. The Federal Fair Housing
Act was put in place to help prevent
landlords from discriminating against
some tenants. You are not allowed to
discriminate against a tenant because
of a disability, their familial status,
sex, religion, national origin, or race.

There are also many states that have
some of their own Fair Housing Rules
that you need to follow. Make sure
that you check in on and adhere to

any local laws that are in place as well.

*Choose a Tenant That Has a Good Credit History*

When picking out tenants, you want to make sure that you look for one who is financially responsible and is likely to pay their rent on time each month. There are two steps that you can do to help check the finances of the tenant and these include:

A. Verify the income.

    a. You want to find a tenant who makes at least three times the amount that you are charging in rent each month.

    b. Ask the tenant for copies of their pay stubs to prove income.

c. Take the time to call the tenant's employer directly to verify information. You can ask about monthly earnings, attendance, how long the person was employed there, and to confirm that they are employed.

B. Run a credit check on them.

a. This is going to show you if the tenant has a history of paying their bills on time.
b. Check out the income to debt ratio the tenant has. They may make three times the rent; but if they have bills that eat up all that income, then you may not see the rent that much.
c. See if the tenant has any bankruptcies, civil

judgments, or prior evictions.

You may have to pay a bit to get these done, but they can reveal a lot of problems about a tenant that you won't be able to find out any other way. You should also write that you are going to verify information and do a credit check for all applicants on the applications. This can scare some of the bad tenants away and can save you a lot of time.

*Do a Criminal Background Check*

Criminal information about your potential tenants is a public record and you can see it at the courthouse in your area. You will be able to find out all the minor and major offenses of the tenant if any. You just need the name and date of birth for your tenant. Check on a valid ID to make sure the tenant is giving you the right information before you do this.

Before you do this, make sure that you understand the rules in your state. For example, in California, you are not able to discriminate against renters for certain criminal convictions. The type of crime is matter as well. A few speeding tickets are probably not enough to refuse someone unless there are other reasons along with this. But a tenant with a violent crime and drug conviction could be an issue and could be dangerous to the other tenants.

There also isn't a nationwide database of these criminal records so doing a thorough background check is hard and can take up a lot of time. Many landlords choose to have a professional company do the work for them to get this done without wasting their own time.

*Look at the Past Rental History of the Tenant*

If you can get this information, spend the time talking to a minimum of two of the tenant's previous landlords. This helps you to know whether the tenant is a problem. The more landlords you find on the list, though, the more likely that the tenant was an issue and you may not want to deal with them. Some questions that you can ask a previous landlord about a potential tenant include:

- Did the tenant spend a lot of time complaining? Did they cause a lot of problems with their neighbors?

- Did they cause a lot of damage to the apartment, besides the normal wear and tear?

- How well did the tenant keep the apartment and was it clean?

- Before they moved in, did the tenant give 30 days' notice? Why did the tenant move out? Did they break the rules or not pay their rent?

- Was the tenant known for paying their rent on time?

Now, there are times when the tenant may be a first-time renter, a recent graduate, or a student; it is possible that they don't have a rental history yet. You can still work with them. Just consider having them put a co-signer on the lease to protect you.

## Choose Tenants Who Are Stable

When you look through the application of the potential tenant, look at their prior addresses and their history of employment. Do you notice that they move a lot or can't seem to keep a job? If you notice that the tenant moves often, this is something they will probably continue and it won't be long before you have a vacancy on your hands. If the tenant does not have a consistent employment history, they may find they are not able to afford the rent in a few months and you have to deal with an eviction.

## Consider How Many Tenants for the Property

The more people you have in each apartment, the more noise, and more wear and tear that can happen to your investment. While there are no really specific rules for how many occupants can be in one room, under the Fair Housing Act, two people for each bedroom is usually reasonable. There are some exceptions to this including:

- State and local law: If your state or your local area has its own housing codes, you need to follow these.

- Size of the dwelling: A bedroom that is 500 sq. ft. can hold more people than a 250 sq. ft.room.

- A unit that has a den and a living room could hold more people than one that does not have.

- Age and number of children: It may be seen as discriminatory to refuse to rent out a one-bedroom house to two adults with an infant. But if you refuse to rent to two adults who have a teenager in one bedroom, that would be reasonable.

- You can choose a maximum number of people that are in an apartment, but you can't have a maximum number of children in the apartment.

- Limitations of the sewer and septic system: If the system capacity can only tolerate a certain amount of people, you can make some rules for this.

*Go with Your Instincts*

You can follow the screenings listed above, but you may find that your instincts are the best way to tell if the tenant is going to be a good one or not. If you spend some time talking to them and find that a tenant seems off or you do not feel comfortable with them for some reason, then trust these instincts. This may be the trick you need to avoid getting a bad tenant into your property.

## Setting Up a Lease

Before the tenant can move into your property, make sure that you get them to sign a lease agreement with you. If a tenant is not willing to sign, this should send up some red flags and you may want to consider picking out someone else. A lease will protect both you and the tenant so not signing one is not in the best interests of either party.

The lease lays out everything that you and the tenant agree on. It will list the address of the property as well as contact information for you in case the tenant needs to get a hold of you. It states the monthly rent and when it is due, along with other charges if the tenant is late on their payments. It also lays out rent's validity period—allowing them to leave without penalties and giving you the freedom to change rent and terms when you want afterward—and it outlines the responsibilities of you as a landlord and of the tenant.

There are often templates that you can pick online to help you write out a good rental agreement. You can also work with a real estate lawyer to write one out. Make sure that all tenants will sign the agreement before you let them move in so that both parties know what to expect from each other and both parties can be protected.

# Chapter 11: Exit Strategies When You Want to Move on

The goal of rental properties is to keep building your empire. You want to finish with the first property and then purchase another, and another, and another. Many people keep growing these until they can make a good passive full-time income, and then even hire a property manager who can do a lot of the work for them. But there are some situations where you may want to leave the rental investment. Some of these reasons include:

- You don't have a good experience with the process: Many people who exit their rental investment do it because they had a bad experience with a tenant. When you begin, realize that having a bad tenant is part of the process. You may just need to get a better screening process in place for your tenants so you make sure you don't have to go through that process again.

- You have some emergency: This could be a family or a medical emergency, a divorce, or something else that takes your attention away from your rental properties. If you just can't keep managing your rental properties, having that exit strategy can make it easier to move on.

- You find that you do not like to be a landlord or do not like to own these rental properties. You tried hard at this business, you analyzed and followed every step that is listed, but once you got into it, you found that you just didn't enjoy being a landlord. This can happen to anyone. There are two options here. You can use your exit strategy and get out of the market, or you can continue to grow your business and deal with the temporary dislike. Once the business has grown enough to support it, consider hiring a property management company to help take care of the work for you. Then you can let them be the landlord instead of doing the work yourself.

- You want to move to bigger and better investments: You may decide to get out of rental properties because you want to work on a different type of investment. If this is the reason that you want to exit the market, then you are heading in the right direction.

- The property you picked ends up costing too much and you don't earn a profit: This problem can occur if you aren't careful with the type of property you picked. Maybe you didn't do an inspection and the property had more work, or you may have thought that the property would earn more income than it does. In any case, you get started on this property and then find you can't make a profit. Even after getting past the first few months of paying off some of the repairs, the property still ends up sinking money and you can't get ahead. When the property is a big loss and you can't earn from it, then it may be the time to exit.

- You decide it is time to retire: After you have been in the rental property business for some time, you may decide that it is time to retire. Some people decide to hand this off to a property manager to ensure they can still earn an income. But others decide that when they retire, they do not want to deal with any of this anymore. If that is your choice, you may want to have an exit strategy to help you get out.

These are just some of the reasons why you may decide that exiting the property rental business is the right decision for you. Having an exit strategy in place from the beginning doesn't mean that you are hoping the project will fail. It simply means that you are preparing in case the investment isn't just right for you or if something else goes wrong.

# Options for Your Exit Strategy

Basically, when you are ready to get out of the rental investment, you simply need to sell or otherwise get rid of the property that you own. There are a few different choices that you can go with when it is time to sell the property, but below are some of the most common options.

*Sell It on MLS as Retail*

The best option to go with to make the highest profit from the sale is to sell your property on MLS. You will need to pay some realtor commissions and deal with closing costs with this, but it can be worth your time.

The first step here is to find a qualified realtor to help you. It is preferable that your rental property is up-to-date and doesn't have any tenants living there at the time. This means that you may have some time when you won't get rental payments while you try to sell that property.

Normal homebuyers are looking for a nice house that is in a nice area. So when you purchase your property to start with, you need to keep in mind that you may try to sell it at some point and choose the area carefully. If your property is in the wrong area or you do not have enough time to fix it up, then it may be best to sell the property to an investor.

## Sell It on MLS to Investors

If you find that the property is not going to work well when you try to sell it as retail, then you may want to still list it on MLS, but cater to investors. If you are doing the selling through MLS at all, then you should still use a realtor and look for one that has some experience working with other investors.

The best way to entice an investor is if the property currently has a tenant inside and the buyer will just be able to earn some cash flow from the moment they purchase it. You need to keep the property in good condition, though, and be honest with the buyer through the whole process. Remember what it was like when you became an investor? Your buyer is an investor here as well and they will want a good deal. This may help you sell the property faster, but remember that the investor will not want to pay the retail price, so you won't make as much with this option.

*Do a For Sale By Owner (FSBO)*

You also have the option to sell and market the property on your own. If you don't feel like using a realtor and spending money on them, you don't have to. You can always sell the property as a For Sale By Owner. There are a lot of options here, such as posting the property's information online or in the newspaper, or using word of mouth to get the information out.

Depending on the property and the situation around you selling the property, you may want to sell the house to traditional homebuyers or sell it to investors. Some sites that you can use to do a For Sale By Owner includeBiggerPockets Marketplace, Craigslist, and FSBO.

*Sell with Owner Financing*

Another tool that you have at your disposal is to sell the property through owner financing. You can market the property using some of the other options above, but then indicate that you also offer owner financing to the right buyer. You get the benefit of setting your own terms, which can open up the gates to other buyers who are less qualified. You may be able to find other investors this way or just open up the door to more potential buyers since you can get some who may not be able to purchase otherwise.

If you want to get out of the investment, but you don't need hard cash right now, this option would be a great one. You will still be holding the papers to the property during this time, but you still collect the cash flow. This basically makes you a note investor.

## Sell the Property Back to the Turnkey Provider If You Bought It That Way

If you have purchased your property from a turnkey provider, then it is possible–in some cases–to sell that property back to the same provider. This is often best as a last option when the other ones are not working out and you really need to get rid of the property. The turnkey provider is not going to purchase the property from you without a huge discount, and you won't recover any of your money selling that way.

With this option, be prepared to lose money on the deal. The shorter the time frame that you hold onto the property, the more money you stand to lose with this one. Yes, purchasing from a turnkey is a good way to purchase a good rental property, but they can only offer these good deals if they have originally purchased them for an even lower price. Remember that when you consider this option.

When you get started with your rental property investments, you should have enough knowledge and preparation that the project will be successful. But sometimes, there are situations that go beyond our control and we decide that it is time to get out of the business. This chapter discussed some of the methods that you can use in order to get rid of the property and move on to other things.

# Chapter 12: What If My Market is Expensive? How to Purchase Rentals in an Expensive Market?

Those who hope to invest in rental properties want to make a long-term passive income. While these rental properties can provide you with a great passive income if you do it right, investing in this manner can be risky. As the housing bubble shows, it is possible to lose a ton of equity in your property if you purchase at the wrong time.No matter what market you invest in, make sure that you start out the process by researching healthy prospects and establishing realistic rent prices and estimated profits.

There are times when the neighborhood you want to invest in will be more expensive. Some whole towns are expensive and you may have trouble even finding the first property you want to go with. Here are some tips that you can follow when you are ready to get into the real estate market with rental property investing:

## Compare the Affordability of the Market

Currently, a lot of first-time homebuyers have trouble purchasing a property—which is why they rent—because some of the most affordable inventory is locked in negative equity. Almost 19% of homeowners right now are underwater on their mortgage, which means they wouldn't be able to sell off the property without having the cash to bring at closing. This low amount of inventory paired with some expensive rents means that most families are stuck renting without much of a chance to purchase a home.

This is a great market for landlords because you will be able to charge higher rates. But it also means that you have to deal with higher purchase prices in some popular areas as well. The median home value on the west coast can be high including Portland ($306,300), Los Angeles ($531,400), and San Francisco ($999,400). These numbers can be seen in other parts of the country as well. A landlord may be able to charge more in rent, but they need significant capital to get into the market and compete with other investors if a reasonable property becomes available.

The good news is that these same kinds of areas are the same ones that renters are willing to pay for. The average rent in Portland, for example, is $1,521 a month, and those in Seattle will pay more than $2,000 on average. If can purchase a property in these areas or others, you will be able to charge a lot more in rent payments each month and make a lot more profit in the process as well.

## Seek out Moderate Pricing

In these expensive areas, a rental property buyer needs to invest a lot of money upfront. Your hopes here are the appreciation of the property over time and you will start to see some positive cash flow from rent. Though some of these places are expensive, the appreciation is still likely there, which means that a long-term investment here will be important for gaining profits. You can consider your realistic returns by subtracting operating costs from the rent income, and then minus the amount you have to pay each month on the mortgage.

Here is a relevant example: A regular mortgage on a property is $500,000 and you put 50% down. The loan has a 4% interest rate, so you will end up paying $2,000 a month, including insurance and property taxes. Imagine this is a property that has 10 units and you could earn $3,500 every month. After you add in your operating expenses at 35%, or $1,225 each month, that gives you a yield of $2,275. Then take the mortgage payment and the owner yields $275 a month. You have to determine if that is enough to make it worth your time.

The more you can invest of your own each month, the lower your mortgage and the higher the monthly returns. Without capital to help you purchase these rentals with cash—which is something that can easily happen in this higher priced areas–you will need to wait to make a purchase or find lower-priced buildings. Make sure you stay away from prize properties because they won't make you any money and they aim for working-class neighborhoods that will charge moderate rents.

Even in these higher-priced areas, you will be able to find a property that meets your needs. It may just take more initial investment and you may have to wait around a bit longer to find the property. You may also need to do some more work on a few properties to get the price reduced to a more affordable level.

## Budget in the Operation Expenses

Before you decide to purchase any rental properties, especially in an expensive area, you need to take the time to plan out your property management strategy. Some owners like to run the whole thing on their own, from signing a lease to working with the tenant and handling any emergencies.

This method can work to help cut out some of your costs. However, it may not be the right approach for you especially if you don't know how to do a lot of the handyman options. If on-call management is not best for you, then you can start to look for some property management companies who can help you out. Just make sure that you take the time to find a good one, and add this into your budget for the rental property.

## Start Your Search as Early as Possible

If you are serious about this new investment, you should start your rental property search as early as possible. In fact, you may want to start this at least three to six months before you are ready to purchase. This may seem like a long time to do your search, but it holds a few advantages to the investor over some other options.

First, it allows you as the investor to really research the market around you and gain a good familiarization of the current values of properties near you. If you jump right into the market and plan to make a purchase in just a few days, then it is hard to know whether you are getting a good deal on a property or not.

If you are searching online for your rental property, don't just rely on the pictures that you see when making a purchase. Go and visit the units and examine some of the comparable sales. You want to walk through each of these properties, especially if you plan to charge enough to reach market rents.

## Work with an Agent

For those who want to purchase rental properties in a more expensive area, you may want to consider working with a buyer's agent. These agents won't cost you anything–the seller takes care of all real estate agent's commissions–and they can provide you with a lot of resources. They know the best areas of the town, they can give you hints on cheaper units coming up, and they can handle all the paperwork when the process is underway. Since they don't cost you anything and they provide you with a lot of great resources, it is worth your time to use these individuals when looking for a property.

## Consider Whether It Is a Good Idea to Live Onsite

One way to select your investment properties is to look for any characteristics that you would want in your own home. Often, the same amenities that appeal to you can also be appealing to your renters. You can look for things such as simple commutes, grocery stores and other shops nearby, and being close to the local areas.

If you purchase a property that you love and would like to live in, it will be more likely to be maintained by the renters as well, and they will also show the right commitment up to keeping this investment.

You can also choose to actually live in the property. If you are just moving to a new area, or if you want to save some of your living costs when you get started with this investment, then consider moving in to one of the properties. Onsite homeowners know about living in those properties and this makes it easier for them to respond to tenants and fix anything that comes up. Buyers who live onsite can get better financing options on the mortgage and can get others to pay for their own living costs, saving some money in these more expensive areas.

# Purchase a Property That Is Already in Good Condition

You may be able to get a property for a good price, but if it will require too much work, you did not get a good deal. You will be required to fix up the property ahead of time, or no tenants will come and live there so you won't make any profits from rent. You want to purchase the property in the best possible conditions that you can.

One thing that you can do here is to invest in an inspection of the property before you close on the home. If the property requires some upgrades—whether you noticed those or they showed up in the inspection—the buyer needs to estimate how much it will cost to do these improvements and if they are affordable before they purchase the property.

If the inspection shows up any issues, you have the options to either walk away from the deal at that point or you can also negotiate some credits from a seller or require that they fix the issue before you purchase. Once it is a done deal, the owner should quickly complete the rest of the upgrades to ensure that the property is safe and ready for tenants to move into.

You should purchase a property that needs a little work. That is the best way to get a good deal on the property and actually make some profits. But if you have to put so much into it that your profits disappear, you are going to be disappointed in the results.

# Really Watch the Costs and Potential Profit

When you purchase these rental properties in an expensive area, you should be careful and really review how profitable the operation will be. Figure out what the unit seller is charging for rent. Figure out how much it will cost to do taxes, insurance, and repair of the property. You should also look at how often tenant turnover occurs and whether the property is already cash flow-positive or if you are going to have to work to improve this. You can check for any property disclosures that show some damages or if there are signs for repairs in the future that can be costly.

You need to go through all these costs and determine if they are the right options for you. You need to walk away from a property because it is not going to actually make you a profit. If the taxes, insurance, upgrades, and mortgage will be higher than what you can reasonably expect to get for monthly rental payments, then it doesn't matter how good of a deal it is. You should not purchase it.

Rental properties can be difficult,to begin with, but when you are in an expensive market, your costs to start will be higher. You can still make a good profit in the process, but you may need to take a bit more time to put together a down payment and you have to work smarter in the market. But, with some good planning and some patience, you can still make money in an expensive market.

# Chapter 13: How Do I Build a Rental Property Empire

Once you have purchased your first property and it seems to be doing well with some positive cash flow from rent, you may want to figure out how you can expand this and make an empire. Over time, you may be able to purchase one property right after another. Each of these can provide you with a positive cash flow that you can use to purchase more properties, or even to help you earn an income. If you are successful, and you purchase enough properties that do well, you can hire a property manager to handle the rentals for you while you earn a full-time passive income and get to accomplish a greater of amount what you want.

The next step here is to come up with a plan and some goals that will help you to build up your rental property empire. Plans and goals are going to work the best when you add specifics and details. If you say that you want to be successful, you have to figure out what that means. Each person defines success in a different manner, some will see it as earning a lot of money, and others are happy if they own a house. The more specific you can make the plans for building your own rental property empire, the easier it will be for you to put those into action.

Below are some of the basics that you can include in your plan when you want to build up a rental property empire.

- How much money do you think the property will generate?

- How much money is needed to start?

- What financing option do you plan to use?

- What type of property will you purchase each time?

- When do you want to purchase the first property, the second property, and so on?

In order to answer these questions, you must take the time to research the market you are going to invest in. If you jump into this option without knowing much about the market, you are not going to see much success with the process. Once you answer the questions above, you will then need to expand out your plan to include things like:

- How will you find a property to purchase?

- How do you plan on managing the property?

- How do you plan to repair that property?

- Do you have any plans for saving money if you need to?

You should write out this plan for each property that you want to purchase. To really help yourself build up a great rental property empire, you need quite a few properties. Then, as you receive rental payments each month, you will be able to earn cash flow from that, while also paying off the loan with each property. Over time, as you pay off everything, you earn more and more profits in the process.

You must start out with your first property. This guidebook has concentrated most of its time on getting you that first rental property. That first property is usually the hardest one to get. You don't know how to work on the market and you should take your time to find it rather than rushing in. That first property is basically a trial run, a learning experience. You will make a lot of mistakes, but you will also learn a lot on the way so that you do better the next time around.

After you have gotten the first property up and running and you have the hang of how things work, you can then start working on the second property. You have a few options here. First, you can save up a bit of your profits each month to help you get enough for a down payment on the second property. Or, you can use the equity you earn in the first property–this property earned equity because of the mortgage payments you make, using your rental properties–to help secure a loan.

This is where a good loan officer can possibly help you out. They can explore different options with you to get you the best rates and options when it is time to work with a second property. You will then follow the same steps again: looking for a good property, making an offer, fixing it all up, and then finding the right tenants. You can then manage that property, get it all set up and making a profit before moving on to your third, fourth, fifth, and more properties.

The more properties you own, the faster your empire is going to grow. This may require some investment, and can even take many years depending on how well you can find properties and earn a profit. But over five or six years, you can start to get a few properties and start that empire. Each property is going to earn you more equity and more profits, which makes it easier to purchase the next property. That first one is always the hardest because you have nothing, but as you move through this process, things get easier.

Over time, you may have enough properties to make a passive income and can leave your regular job to take this on full-time. Even better, you may have enough properties that you can hire a property management company to handle the day-to-day operations, while you take the rental payments as a passive income and just enjoy life. And that is the ultimate goal with your empire: to turn this into a passive income so you can make as much as you want while someone else takes care of it all.

It may be a rough start with the first property, but no matter how hard it is, just keep going since you are still learning. Each property that you pursue after this will be easier to handle, and you will find that this is a very profitable way to make money.

# Chapter 14: Tips to Help Every Beginner Get Started and See Success with Their Investment

As a beginner, you are probably excited to get out there and purchase your first property. You have big dreams of getting that property, finding your first tenants, and earning a check. But there is a lot of work that goes into one of these investments and you want to make sure that you are doing it the right way. Here are some of the best tips that you can follow as a beginner to ensure you can see this rental property investment become as profitable as possible.

## Always Have Reasonable Expectations

You may have heard the stories of someone who got into rental property investing and then a year later, they were making $400,000 a year while vacationing. This is not a reasonable expectation to have. Over time, as you purchase more properties and your rents increase, you may be able to do this with the help of a property manager. But you cannot go from nothing to high wages in just a few months. And if someone tells you that you can, then you should run the other way from that scam.

While it is a good idea to have the goal of a positive cash flow, you should never expect that after a year in the market you can already live the high life. For the first few years at least, these rental properties are probably going to be part-time and side incomes that you can use to help build your empire. You won't be able to make the big money until much later on. Be sure to keep all your expectations in check so that you make reasonable decisions about your properties and can actually earn an income.

## Do the Research About the Market Ahead of Time

You should never just get into this type of investment without doing some research. Many investors are reckless having known that there can be a passive income in rental properties. So they will go and find their first property without knowing what the market prices are, how much they will have to spend to fix it up, or how much they can charge in rent. They easily spend too much and they have to fix too much on the property. The rental payments may not be enough to cover the costs they incur.

It is always important to take the time to learn about the market and everything that you need to do to make rental properties as profitable as possible. You can benefit from watching the market for two or three months before even looking at loans or looking for a specific property to purchase. This helps you to know the market and what you can reasonably expect when you get into it. Those who don't rush into this investment are the ones who have the most luck and see results with their rental property empire.

## Always Inspect the Property

An inspection can make a big difference on whether or not you purchase the property. You can do an inspection and get a good idea on whether the property is actually worth the money you are going to spend or not. If you find a major issue in the property, you still have time to back out without spending anything. Or, to help you get the property without spending as much money, you can ask the seller to shoulder the repair cost or just deduct whatever cost that will incur from what you owe to the seller.

Even if the inspection doesn't find anything major that you need to fix or be concerned about, you can still use it as a way to help you determine what needs to be done to make the home more presentable. You can work with a general contractor to see what things will cost, such as adding in an extra bedroom or fixing the plumbing, so you can add this into your costs when determining the profitability of the property.

## Find a Good Balance Between Your Earnings and the Effort You Put in

When you get started with this kind of investment, you need to figure out how much work you want to put in. Do you plan to work with a property management firm or do the work yourself? This will matter because it can take up either more of your time or more of your potential profits. Not being careful with either one can be a hassle.

Some landlords decide that they want to take on all the work of the property and be more hands-on. That allows them to keep more of their profits in their own pockets. But taking care of even one property—much less multiple units at once—can get really time-consuming to work on. If you have another job, kids, a family, and other obligations, you may find that all of your free time is taken up with the properties.

If you don't have the time and energy to be a hands-on landlord, you will want to hire a property management team. This helps you to still make an income, but not have to spend your whole life at the property. While it is fine to do some of the work on your own to save money, you don't want to end up spending all day at the property only to make a few hundred dollars each month.

# Know All the Rules in Your Area (Both Federal and State Laws)

Depending on where you live, there will be different federal and state laws that will say what you are responsible for and what you are liable for as a landlord. Before you sign a lease with any tenant, you are expected to know all of these laws. You cannot claim ignorance when something happens.

You need to spend time reading up on the laws and regulations for landlords in your area to make sure that you don't miss out on anything. You can also check up on the responsibilities for the tenants as well to make sure that you understand what your job is and what needs to be done by the tenant. This can take some time, but it is much better to do this now rather than having to spend time in court later because you missed out on something. If you are uncertain about a rule or something similar, then you should consider seeking legal counsel to help keep you safe.

## Check That Your Leases Are Legal

You need to be extremely careful about the kind of lease that you are writing up for your tenants. There are certain legal terms allowed and certain ones that should be avoided to ensure that your lease is legal and that you are protected if it is time to evict the tenant from the property. If you make a mistake on the lease, then it is very difficult to litigate when the tenant violates the terms, even if you verbally agreed to certain things.

You should consider hiring an attorney to help you out. They can draw up a lease that is legal and will protect you and the tenant according to the laws in your local area. You can use this lease for all of your tenants and it can be used to protect you when things go wrong with them. You can ask the lawyer to help you write out the terms and the lease in a way that you can add in the names, dates, rent, and other details about the agreement so it is unique for each tenant.

# Work with a Real Estate Agent

We have mentioned this a few times in this guidebook, but when you are looking for the perfect rental property, you should consider hiring a real estate agent to help you get your first property. You could try to do the work on your own, but since a real estate agent doesn't charge you for their services as the buyer, it is often better to work with one to get the job done.

Your real estate agent can work with you from the moment you start looking until you close on the property. They can help you find some of the best investment properties because they have more networks and connections than you might have. Then, when you are ready to purchase the property, they can do the paperwork, help you with negotiations, and put the right contingencies into place so you can walk away from the deal if things go wrong. Your agent can help with inspections, any renegotiations, and everything else until you close on the property and have the keys in your hand.

Getting started in rental properties is a great way to put your money to work for you. It takes some investment and risks in the beginning. But, over time, you are going to earn a steady paycheck each month, especially if you get that investment to grow into more than one property and provide you with a growth in equity as well. There is no investment quite like rental property investing, and these tips will give you a chance to get ahead in the market!

# Conclusion

Thank you for making it through to the end of *Rental Property Investing*. Let's hope it was informative and able to provide you with all of the tools you need to achieve your goals whatever they may be.

Once you have made up your mind in what you are looking for in a property, the next step is to get into the rental property investing business. This is an exciting way to help you earn money on the side, or even as a full-time income, without entering the stock market or worrying about any of the things that happen in that investment. Rental properties can benefit you in so many ways. They help you to earn an income and to earn equity and you have the option to sell the property when you are done at a higher price–thanks to the rise in property values–so you can make even more money in the process.

This guidebook took some time to discuss rental property investing and all the steps that you need to follow to get started with this type of investment. Starting out in this kind of investment, though, is a long journey before you become a successful rental property investor. It also takes some money to get started with and there are some risks. But if you really do your research and put in the time and effort to find a good property, this can be a great way to make some money in this type of investment.

When you are looking at some of your options for investing and you are not sure where to begin, make sure to check out this guidebook and learn more about rental property investing today.

Finally, if you find this book useful in any way, a review on Amazon is always appreciated!